Page04
REY MYSTERIO VS. CHAVO GUERRERO

Page16
KANE VS

Page26
JOHN MORRISON VS. CM PUNK

Page34
BATISTA VS. GREAT KHALI

REY MYSTERIO VS. CHAVO GUERRERO

Chavo Guerrero destroyed Rey Mysterio's knee, and nearly his career, in October 2006 in a vicious "I Quit" Match on *SmackDown*. At *SummerSlam*, the returning masked marvel would face Guerrero one-on-one with retribution on his mind.

This match was made by *SmackDown* assistant general manager Vickie Guerrero, despite her past involvement regarding Mysterio's injury. Vickie has been an impartial and unbiased voice to complement general manager Theodore Long, much to the dismay of her nephew-in-law Chavo, and the satisfaction of the fans.

What would Rey have in store for the man who attempted to end his career? Could the master of the 619 avenge the injury that had kept him out of ring action for almost a full year? Or would Chavo Guerrero concentrate a sadistic attack on Rey's surgically repaired knee, forever grounding the high-flying Superstar?

"Well, here we are, Cole, about to witness this tense matchup between Rey Mysterio and Chavo Guerrero."
"It's going to be a brutal match, partner. There is no love lost between these two men!"
"It's been a long time since we've heard this music, JBL!"
"He's back, Cole, and he is getting a huge reaction from this crowd!"
WARRIOR
"Here comes Chavo Guerrero. This is a man who turned on his best friend and put him out of action for nearly 12 months."
"He didn't just put him out of action, Cole. He nearly ended Mysterio's career!"
"It looks like Rey has been spending some time in the sun bed during his recuperation!"
"Rey Mysterio is well known for his unique look, and he certainly looks pretty unique tonight!"

"Who does he think he is, Cole? The Silver Surfer?"
"I think he looks great, JBL, and I think the crowd here agrees with me!"

"You know, Cole, I might not like Rey Mysterio, but I am sure glad that he has returned to WWE!"
"That makes two of us, partner!"

"Rey Mysterio is obviously very happy to be back here at *SummerSlam*!"
"He needs to forget about the fans, though, and concentrate on what is really important, his opponent, Chavo Guerrero!"
"I'm pretty sure that that is all Rey Mysterio has been thinking about since Chavo put him out of action in that brutal "I Quit" Match last October!"

"Here we go, Cole. After six months of build-up, these two Superstars are about to face off."
"You could cut the tension with a knife here, JBL!"

"Rey goes straight for a monkey flip, sending Chavo to the outside!"
"We are going to see a lot of *lucha libre*-style action in this match, Cole."
"Mysterio with a suicide plancha over the top rope and onto a helpless Chavo Guerrero! That is what you call a high-risk move!"
"Mysterio needs to be careful. His knee can't be 100 percent healed yet!"
"Mysterio sends Chavo back into the ring, and hits him with a springboard seated senton!"
"Mysterio's knee looks fine from where I'm sitting, JBL."

"Ha ha! Look at this though, Cole. Guerrero is going straight after the knee!"
"That injured knee is like a big red target to Guerrero, and you can bet he will use every trick in the book to try and re-injure Mysterio!"
"Of course he will, Cole. He is a Guerrero after all, and those boys have a mean streak as wide as the Mississippi!"
"Guerrero is cranking away on Mysterio's knee. That joint is just not meant to bend like that!"
"Mysterio makes his way back up to a vertical base. And wow! What an enziguri kick!"
"I just don't know how Rey Mysterio does it, Cole!"

"But look, JBL! Chavo Guerrero goes straight back to the injured knee!"
"The Boston Crab manoeuvre will be so painful for Rey Mysterio, he needs to get to the ropes!"

"And he does, JBL! Chavo Guerrero has gone to the outside! What could he be doing?"
"Here comes Rey Mysterio! What a move to the outside!"

"Both men are back on the inside, and Rey Mysterio hits Guerrero with another seated senton!"
"The tide seems to be turning in Mysterio's favour here, Cole!"

"Mysterio with another high-risk move! A moonsault from the top rope!"
"He caught Guerrero perfectly with that manoeuvre!"

"Mysterio is climbing the ropes again. He may be going to the well once too often here, Cole!"
"You're right, JBL. Mysterio went for the cross-body block, but there was no one home!"

"You know what this move is, Cole? It's the Gory Bomb, invented by Chavo's grandfather, the late, great Gory Guerrero!"
"Not may people get up from that move, JBL!"
"But look! Mysterio has Chavo in the ropes!"
"It could be 619 time here, Cole!"

"Mysterio goes for it!"
"But look at that, Cole! Guerrero ducked out of the way!"
"Guerrero has Rey set up for the Three Amigos suplexes!"
"This move was made famous by Chavo's late uncle, WWE Hall of Famer Eddie Guerrero!"
"Just how in the blue hell did Rey Mysterio escape from that manoeuvre, Cole?"
"I don't know, partner! But he has Chavo set up for the 619 again!"
"And this time he hits hit!"

The referee counts to three and Mysterio has won it!
"I have to hand it to Mysterio. That was one hell of a comeback!
"You can bet Mysterio has been thinking about this moment for a long time!"
"Mysterio looks overwhelmed to have won that match, Cole!"
"He deserved to win the match, although at times it looked like Chavo Guerrero was in complete control!"
"I think it is pretty obvious that the crowd here tonight wanted Mysterio to come out of this match victorious."
"And our great fans got exactly what they paid for, partner!"

KANE VS. FINLAY

With a little convincing from the "Big Red Monster" himself, the WWE Chairman, Mr. McMahon, elected to honour Kane's request to meet Finlay one-on-one, and it would happen at the "Biggest Party of the Summer," *SummerSlam*.

Kane had been stalking the Finlay ever since the belligerent Irishman accidentally knocked several ounces of scalding coffee onto Kane two weeks before on *SmackDown*. That night, the former WWE Champion dispensed of Finlay, wildly thrashing him throughout the arena hallways. Later on, however, Finlay assaulted the "Big Red Monster" using his dependable ally, the shillelagh. Finlay did the same one week later during Kane's title match against the then-World Heavyweight Champion, the Great Khali. Interrupting the behemoths' *WrestleMania 23* rematch, Finlay may have caused further damage to his enemy's taped ribs, but it also added gallons of fuel to Kane's ever-burning fire.

What began with a little incident involving a cup of coffee weeks ago will now culminate at *SummerSlam*, as two of *SmackDown*'s most violent Superstars face off. Who would emerge the victor in this rugged war? Would *SummerSlam* turn out to be the biggest beatdown of the summer for Finlay? Or would Kane find himself one shillelagh shot away from being robbed of the revenge he wanted?

"Here comes the Fighting Irishman, Finlay!"
"They don't get much tougher than the former United States Champion."
"And you have to always keep an eye out for that little critter, Hornswoggle!"
"And here is his opponent, the "Big Red Monster," Kane!"
"This is going to be brutal, partner! There's no two ways about it.
"The referee calls for the bell, and the match is underway!"
"Kane delivers a huge right hand to Finlay that almost knocks him all the way back to Ireland!"
"And he follows up with a huge elbow drop. Kane is just so powerful!"
"It's high impact all the way with Kane. Once he has just a little momentum behind him, there is no stopping this guy!"

"Kane has Finlay backed up into the corner. And he delivers a huge knee to the Irishman's mid-section."
"How much of a factor do you think Kane's injured ribs will be in this match, JBL?"
"Broken ribs make it so hard to breath. Kane will be tiring out pretty soon!"
"From this angle, you can clearly see Kane's heavily taped ribs, the result of a brutal shillelagh attack at the hands of Finlay!"
"And there you have it, Cole! Finlay is working over those injured ribs with some stiff boots!"
"I can only imagine the pain that Kane is in right now!"

"That's because you are too much of a wimp to ever set foot in the ring!"
"I know just where I belong, partner, and that is this side of the announce desk!"
"It looks like Finlay is going for a single-leg Boston Crab here, Cole!"

"Finlay has it locked in! Kane may have to submit right here!"
"That is really going to be hurting Kane's ribs, Cole!"

"Finlay has Kane down in the corner! And he drops all his weight down onto Kane's rib cage!"
"Finlay has a great game plan here. He has spotted Kane's weakness and is going to concentrate on that area!"
"What's this, JBL? Finlay is looking for something under the ring!"
"It's Hornswoggle, Cole! That little fleabag has been under the ring all along!"

"Finlay and Hornswoggle are in the ring, JBL!"
"Hornswoggle may be the Cruiserweight Champion, but I don't like his chances against Kane! And look! Kane has just sat up!"
"Kane climbs to the top rope! And flies through the air to connect with a huge clothesline!"
"No one in this business is as agile as Kane, considering his size!"
"What impact on that manoeuvre! Kane almost beheaded Finlay!"
"Let me tell you, Cole. I have been on the receiving end of that move, and it doesn't tickle!"

"Look, Cole! Hornswoggle is trying to get back under the ring!"
"Do you blame him? Kane looks like he might try and eat the little fellow!"
"He's not going to eat him, Cole! He's going to Chokeslam him straight to hell!"
"I don't know which would be worse!"

"Finlay makes the save... but Kane has him set up for the Chokeslam, too!"
"But there you see the experience of Finlay, while the referee wasn't looking, he hit Kane with a low blow!"
"Finlay goes for the pin, but only gets the two count!"
"That looked like a slow count to me!"
"Kane is back up to his feet and hits Finlay with a huge uppercut!"
"That was a thunderous shot from Kane!"
"Finlay is backing off!"
"He's going to the outside, Cole!"

"Hornswoggle has handed him a shillelagh!"
"Finlay with a wicked-looking shot to the already-injured ribs of Kane!"

"But it only seems to have angered the "Big Red Monster!"
"Kane Chokeslams him straight to hell!"

"Kane with the cover! One... two... three! It's all over! Kane wins! Kane wins!"
"Both men will be feeling that match for a month, Cole! What a war!"

JOHN MORRISON VS. CM PUNK

CM Punk not only survived John Morrison's 15 Minutes of Fame Challenge on *ECW*, he defeated the ECW Champion. Punk's big win earned him a chance at Morrison's ECW Championship at *SummerSlam*.

Morrison, the self-proclaimed guru of greatness, had pondered if Punk could handle his 15 Minutes of Fame Challenge. He announced that the end was near for Punk, and that no one would remember his name. Punk countered, promising no one would ever forget the name CM Punk. The "Straight-edge Superstar" proved Morrison wrong, winning his chance at ECW gold at *SummerSlam*.

It's Punk's time to shine, as he knocks on the door of Morrison's so-called palace of wisdom. Punk would face Morrison at *SummerSlam* in East Rutherford, N.J. Would Morrison – the new face of Extreme – prove his fame is infinite? Or could Punk prove his focus and dedication are deserving of the ECW Championship?

"Well here we go, Joey! The ECW Championship on the line at *SummerSlam*!"
"I can't wait for this one, Tazz! The arrogant John Morrison taking on the future of ECW, CM Punk!"

"You know what, Joey? John Morrison has every right to be arrogant. Look at this guy!"
"I can't deny that he is one hell of an athlete. But the way he carries himself, in my opinion, is not the way a champion should!"
"Well, I doubt Morrison gives a damn about your opinion, Joey!"

"You may be right, Tazz, but do you think he cares about the boos he is getting from this crowd?"
"He certainly isn't the crowd favourite in this match, and that's for sure!"

"Now, here is a guy who acts like a champion!"
"I hate to say it, but I have to agree with you there, partner!"

"CM Punk is getting a huge reaction from the crowd here tonight! This could very well be the biggest match of his young career!"
"Punk has a great opportunity here, no doubt. I just wonder if he is ready to step up to the plate and take on someone with as much experience as John Morrison."

"John Morrison looks super-confident tonight!"
"You're right, Tazz. He certainly doesn't look intimidated by CM Punk!"

"On the flip side, I don't think I have ever seen CM Punk looking more focused!"
"A win here tonight would be huge for this young Superstar!"
"The referee rings the bell and here we go!"

"CM Punk takes the champion down with a perfect armdrag!"
"Punk may be one of the most technically sound Superstars in ECW right now, Joey!"

"Punk with the Dropkick! Did you see the height he got on that, Tazz?"
"He caught Morrison right in the mouth!"

"Now Morrison is on the offensive with some huge right hands!"
"The momentum in this match is swinging back and forth like an out of control pendulum!"

"The champion is trying to wear down the challenger with some sort of rear chinlock here!"
"CM Punk really needs to escape from this hold, or he could be in real trouble!"
"OH MY GOD! Did you see that, Tazz? A brutal kick to the back of the champ's head!"
"Wow, Joey! CM Punk has such educated feet. He can hit you from out of nowhere!"
"It looks like Punk is getting ready to fly. This is a very high-risk strategy!"
"Punk hits the cross-body block from the top rope!"

"And look at this follow up! A real hard Clothesline!"
"That almost took Morrison's head clean off!"
"Punk has this match won! Make the pin, Punk! Make the pin!"
"Morrison just hit CM Punk with a blatant low blow!"
"He can't do that! That's cheating!"
"It's only cheating if you get caught, Joey!"
"The referee never saw it! John Morrison has got the three count and retained his title! This makes me sick, Tazz!"
"All is fair in love and war, Joey. It's about time you learned that!"

BATISTA
★★★ VS. ★★★
GREAT KHALI

Not often in his WWE career has Batista had to step into the ring with a man who's taller, bigger and perhaps even stronger than he is. But if he hopes to regain one of sports-entertainment's richest prizes, *SmackDown*'s "Animal" must do precisely that when he faces the Great Khali for the World Heavyweight Championship at *SummerSlam*.

It was just weeks before *SummerSlam* when a fortunate stroke of luck befell Batista. Just six days before *The Great American Bash*, he was set to face Khali one-on-one at the pay-per-view. But then an injured Edge was forced to relinquish the World Heavyweight Championship, and a 20-Man Battle Royal was held on *SmackDown* to determine the new champion. Batista was thought to be the odds-on favourite by many, until he ran into a force that even nature can't seem to stop: a 7-foot-3, 420-pound Punjabi powerhouse. Khali cleaned house and eliminated Kane and the "Animal" to win the gold.

The most dangerous animal is one whose back is against the wall. It's not a situation Batista is in often, but it's one that usually sees him come through. Would Batista be the man to dethrone The Great Khali, or would the Punjabi powerhouse retain his title and remain the one Superstar on *SmackDown*?

"Well, Cole, are you ready for tonight's main event?"
"The Great Khali versus the "Animal" Batista! This is going to be a battle for the ages!"

"Just look at Khali, Cole! This guy is huge! I don't think I have ever seen an athlete with his power!"
"Batista is sure going to have his work cut out for him tonight! Although we did see that Batista can take the big man down last week on *SmackDown*!"

"And here comes the challenger, Batista! Just listen to the reaction of the crowd, JBL!"
"I can't deny it, Cole. Batista is a real fan favourite."
"And he looks really fired up tonight, John! He is desperate to win back the title!"
"He can be as fired up as he likes, Cole. It doesn't mean a thing unless he can take the champion off his game!"
"I don't think I have ever seen Batista dwarfed by an opponent before!"
"This Khali dwarfs everybody, Cole! He must be five times your size!"

"The bell rings, and these two giants lock up in the centre of the ring! Look at Khali, he just pushed Batista away like he was a cruiserweight!"
"Batista is going to have to change his tactics here. He can't rely on overpowering his opponent in this match."

"Khali shoots Batista into the ropes and hits him with a huge clothesline!"
"That must have felt like running into a brick wall, Cole!"

"Khali just delivered a huge boot right into Batista's face!"
"Khali has been totally dominant thus far in the match!"

"It looks like Khali might be setting Batista up for that devastating nerve hold he likes so much!"
"I don't see this match going much longer if Khali can apply that move!"

"Just look at Khali, stalking his opponent!"
"He is like a wild animal just toying with his prey!"

"Khali has it locked in! Batista may be forced to tap out right here!"
"This hold is so painful! The pressure applied to the trapezius muscles cuts off the blood supply to the brain and can send you to sleep in a second!"

"Batista is desperately trying to get back to his feet!"
"He really needs to break this hold if he wants any chance at regaining the championship!"

"Khali is just so strong! He has forced Batista back down to his knees!"
"Batista somehow makes it to the ropes, and Khali is forced to break the hold!"

"Khali reverses the Irish Whip and Batista is met with another huge boot to the face!"
"Batista has not been able to mount any offence in this match so far, Cole!"

"Oh no, JBL! It looks like Khali is going back to that nerve hold!"
"I'll put my neck on the line here and say that if he locks this move in again, the match will be over!"

"Batista has blocked it! Look at the strength being displayed by the "Animal" here!"
"I don't believe it, Cole! How is Batista doing it?"
"Batista is overpowering the giant! I have never seen this before!"
"Take a look at Khali's face! He can't believe it either, Cole!"
"Batista breaks the hold and shoots into the ropes!!"
"Batista is going for the spear! Will it be enough to take the big man off his feet?"

"Spear! Batista spears Khali and takes him down for the first time in this match!"
"That impact was like two trucks hitting each other head on at full speed, Cole!"

"Wait Cole! Khali is back on his feet!"
"He has Batista up for the double-handed Chokeslam!"

"Khali hits the Khali Bomb! This match is over!"
"Khali goes for the cover! One... two... Batista kicks out! Batista is still in this thing, JBL!"

"Khali can't believe Batista kicked out! He has gone to the outside and picked up a steel chair! Oh my god! What a chair shot from Khali!"

"The referee has seen him though and taken the chair off him! Khali has been disqualified!"
"Check this out, Cole! Batista has the chair and he's going crazy with it!"
"Batista has snapped! He is wailing away on Khali with that chair!"
"Well, I guess that is one way to take the giant down!"

"Someone get security out here! Batista has lost it!"
"Can you blame him, JBL? Khali got himself intentionally disqualified and has kept the title!"
"This war is not over, Cole! I am sure these two men will meet again somewhere down the road!"
"Khali could not defeat the "Animal" here tonight at *SummerSlam*! I can't wait for these guys to have a rematch! That's it from us here at *SummerSlam*! We'll see you at *SmackDown*!"

summerslam RESULTS

WWE Champion **John Cena def. Randy Orton**

Triple H def. King Booker

Batista def. World Heavyweight Champion **The Great Khali** (DQ, Khali retains)

Rey Mysterio def. Chavo Guerrero

ECW Champion **John Morrison def. CM Punk**

Intercontinental Champion **Umaga def. Mr. Kennedy and Carlito**

Kane def. Finlay

Beth Phoenix wins Divas Battle Royal